I0488569

Mandalas for Relaxation Colouring Book

By April Wood

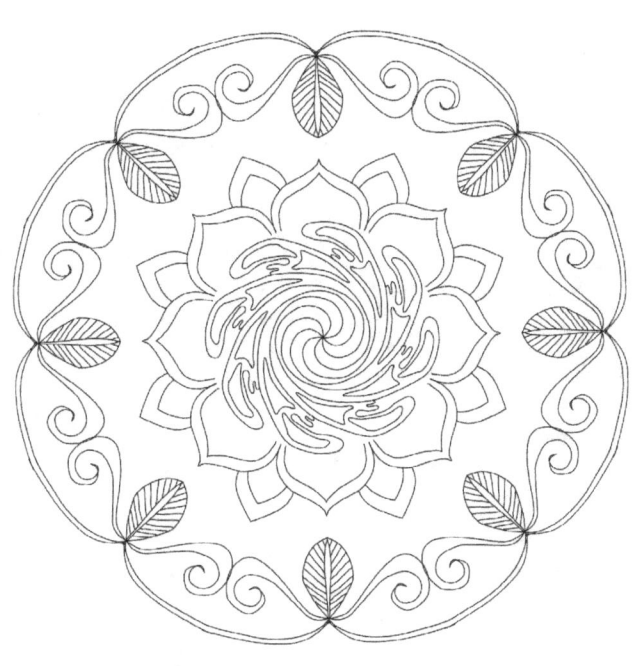

Introduction

Colouring has been shown time and time again to be of benefit not only for children, but for adults as well as a means of relaxing, reducing stress, and having some down time.

This book has been designed to help you be the happiest version of you possible. Each mandala has an explanation of why it has been included, which you are able to reflect on while you colour it in. Or you can give it your own meaning- that is completely ok too!

I have provided you with the basic images, they are now yours to fill with colour, life, and joy.

There is a blank mandala at the end of this colouring book which will allow you make your own mandala if you so choose.

Happy Colouring!

All images and text within this book is copyright to
April Wood, please only reproduce for personal use.

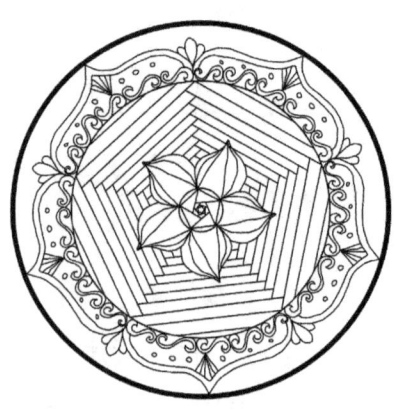

Change

Change is the only thing that is guaranteed in life. How do you cope with change? What things could you do to help you adjust to new challenges? Build a strong foundation to make yourself more resiliant, and you will flourish.

Calm in the storm

Within the craziness of life, there will always be a calm if you take the time to look for it.

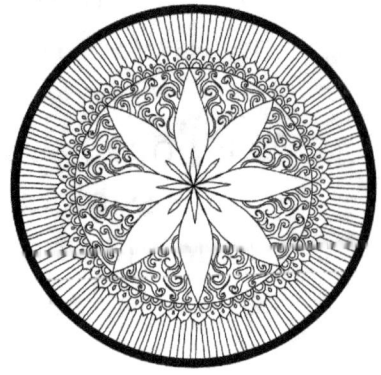

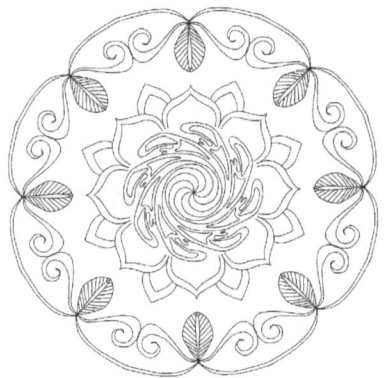

A Rose for You

A rose is a symbol of love, friendship, companionship, grief, forgiveness, desire, and appreciation among other things. This rose is for you, it is the versatile flower that is full of love.

Let Love In

Sometimes it can be hard to open our hearts if we have been hurt in the past. This mandala is about opening those gates, letting down those barriers and allowing the love flow from those around us to our central core.

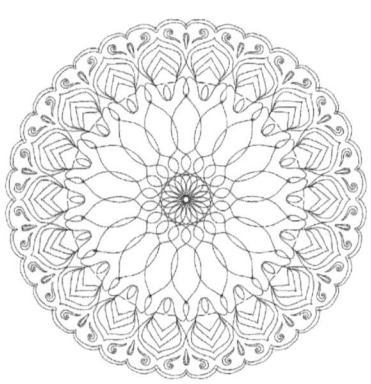

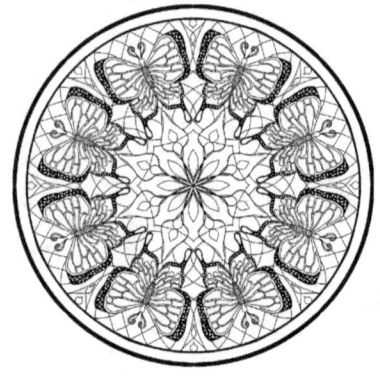

Free like a Butterfly

Fly free little butterfly! Be free to be you, free yourself from the constraints that others set on you, live the life that you want, and feel wonderful doing it!

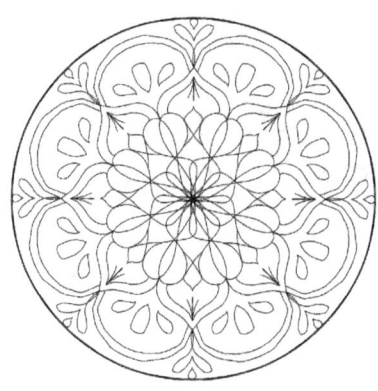

Eye of the World

Everyone views the world through their own lens. Life experiences help to shape how we are and who we are, this is a reminder that two people going through the same thing may have two very different experiences due to their history and differing morals/ethics.

Reaching Out

When we have inner turmoil, many people just go internal and don't reach out for help, this is about reaching out during those times, not weathering the storm on your own.

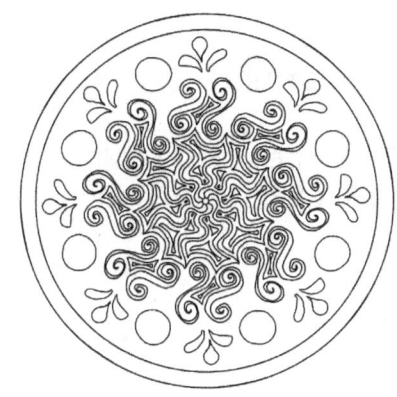

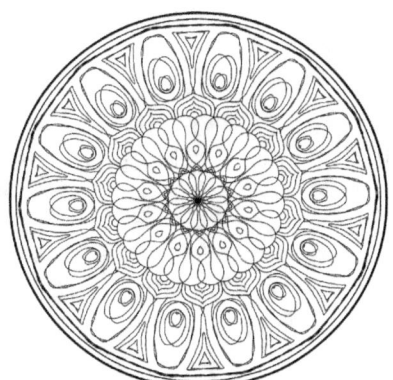

Make your Mark on the World

How will you make your mark on the world? What will you do that will make a difference? This doesn't need to be a huge change that will impact thousands, just helping someone to cross the road, or smiling at a stranger can change their day for the better.

Bubbling with Joy

When you allow yourself to bloom you will bubble with joy, it will be infectious and inspiring to all those around you.

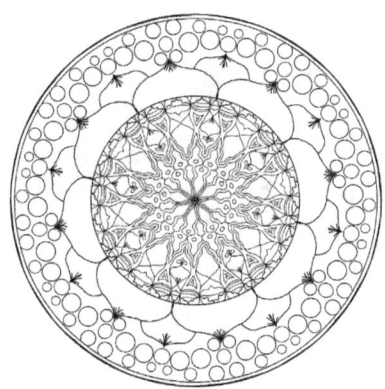

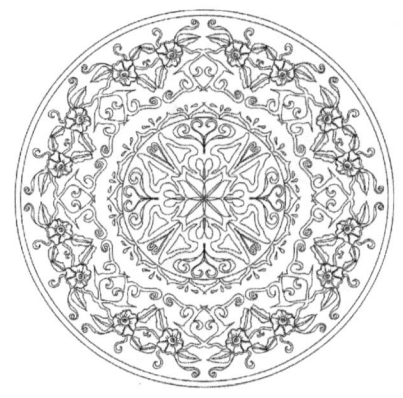

Fertile Ground

Only with fertile ground is a garden able to grow and flourish. What are you doing to make your mind a place for you to grow and flourish?

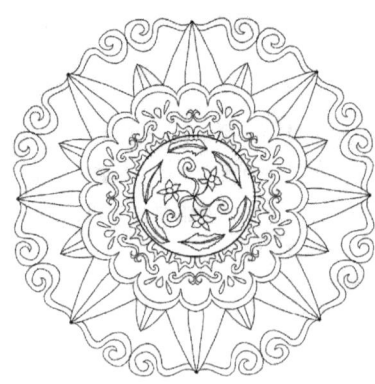

Your Direction

Take stock of where you are, where you are going, and where you want to go. Are you on track? What do you need to do to make sure you are filling your heart with joy?

Star bright

Everyone shines when they are given the right tools. What tools do you need to help you shine your brightest?

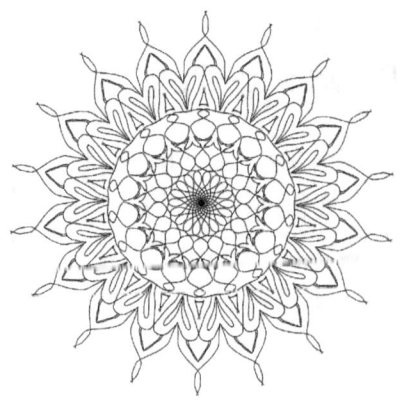

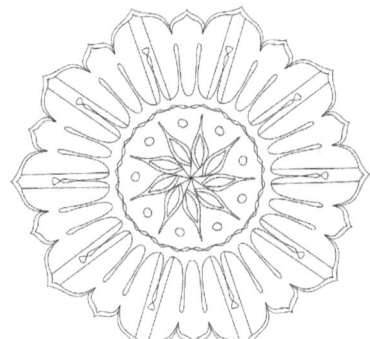

Simplify

Sometimes you need to just clean out all the clutter and just keep things simple.

Bursting Free

A flower breaks free of the constraints set around it. You too can burst free into full bloom when you give yourself the nourishment you need.

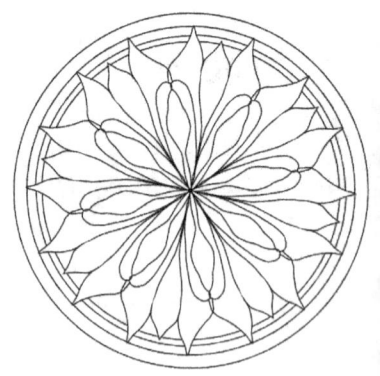

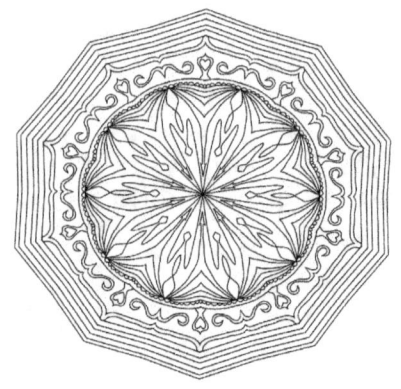

Stop

Take time to rest. Take time out. Take time for YOU!

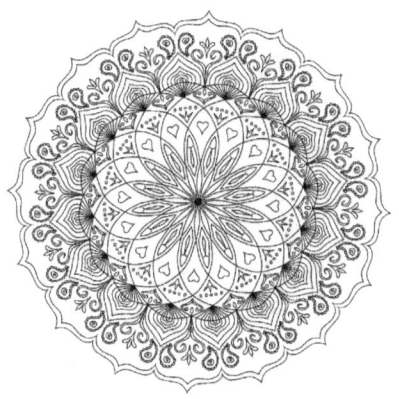

Surrounded by love

Who surrounds you? Do they support you? Do they encourage you to be the best you that you can be?

Fill in the Blank

Your life is much like a blank canvas, it is up to you as to how you fill up your time, heart, and life. Try to make sure you are filling it with joy and love.

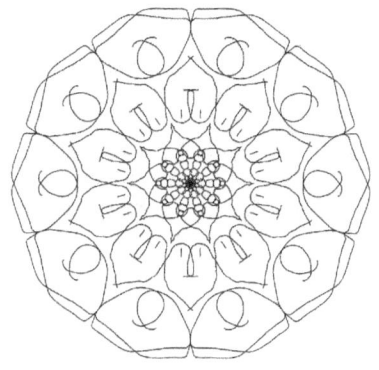

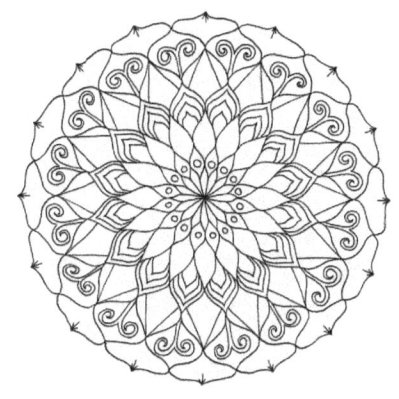

The Layers of You

Within each of us are many, many different layers of US. We have the professional, the personal, the partner, the parent, the child, and the sibling to name a few. Which layers do you prioritise, which need more nurturing?

Warmth of the Sun

This is a reminder that just like plants need the sun to grow, you need love, acceptance and plenty of warmth in your life for you to grow and flourish.

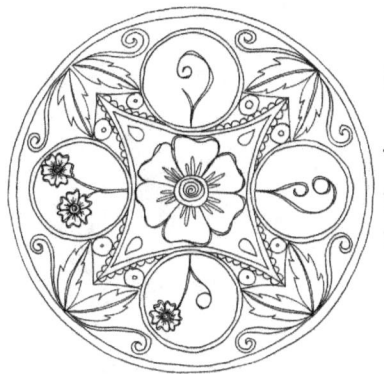

Growth

This mandala is all about the continuous cycle of life, a reminder that there will always be a time when you are struggling, there will be a time when you will again be in full bloom.

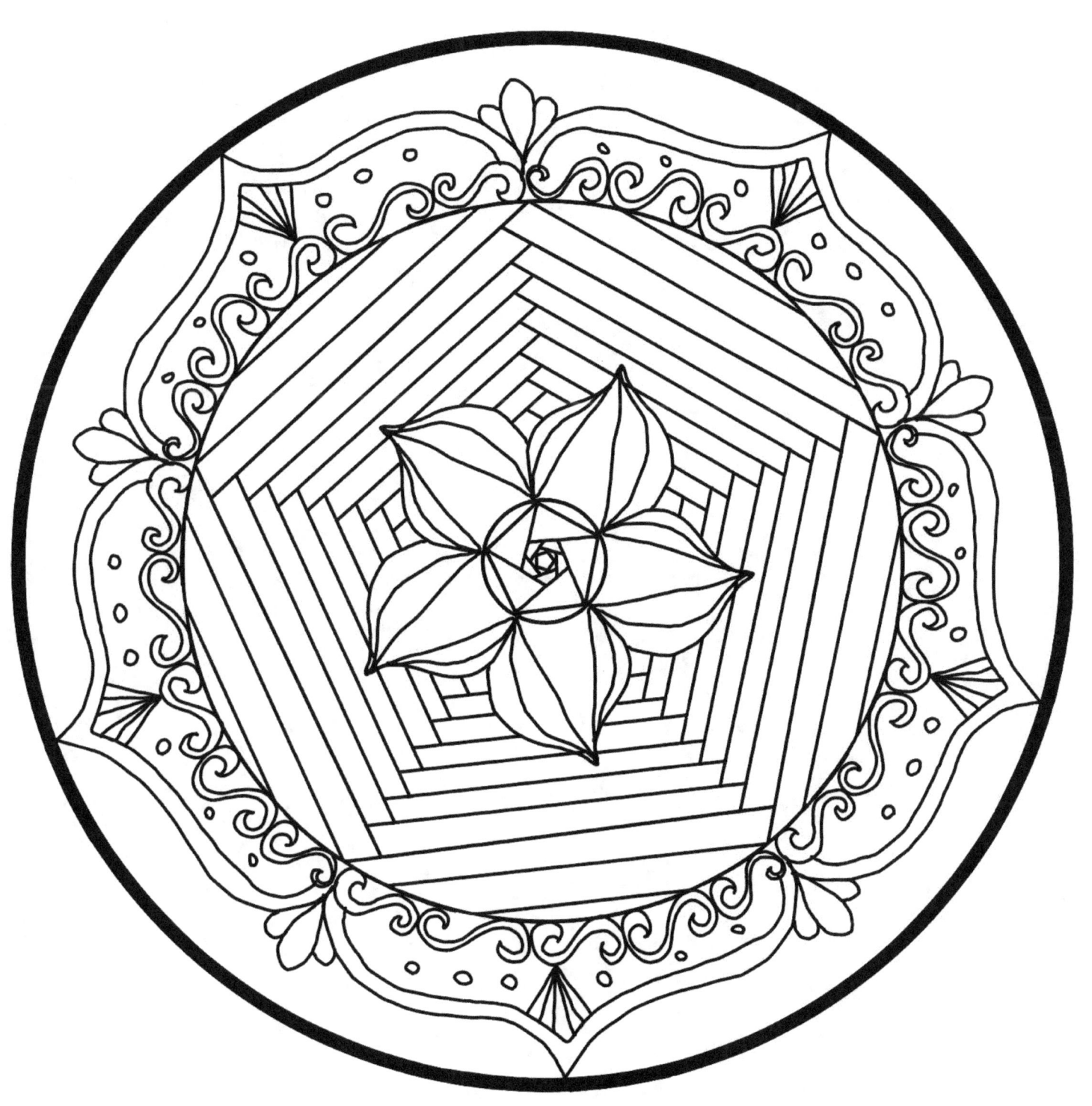

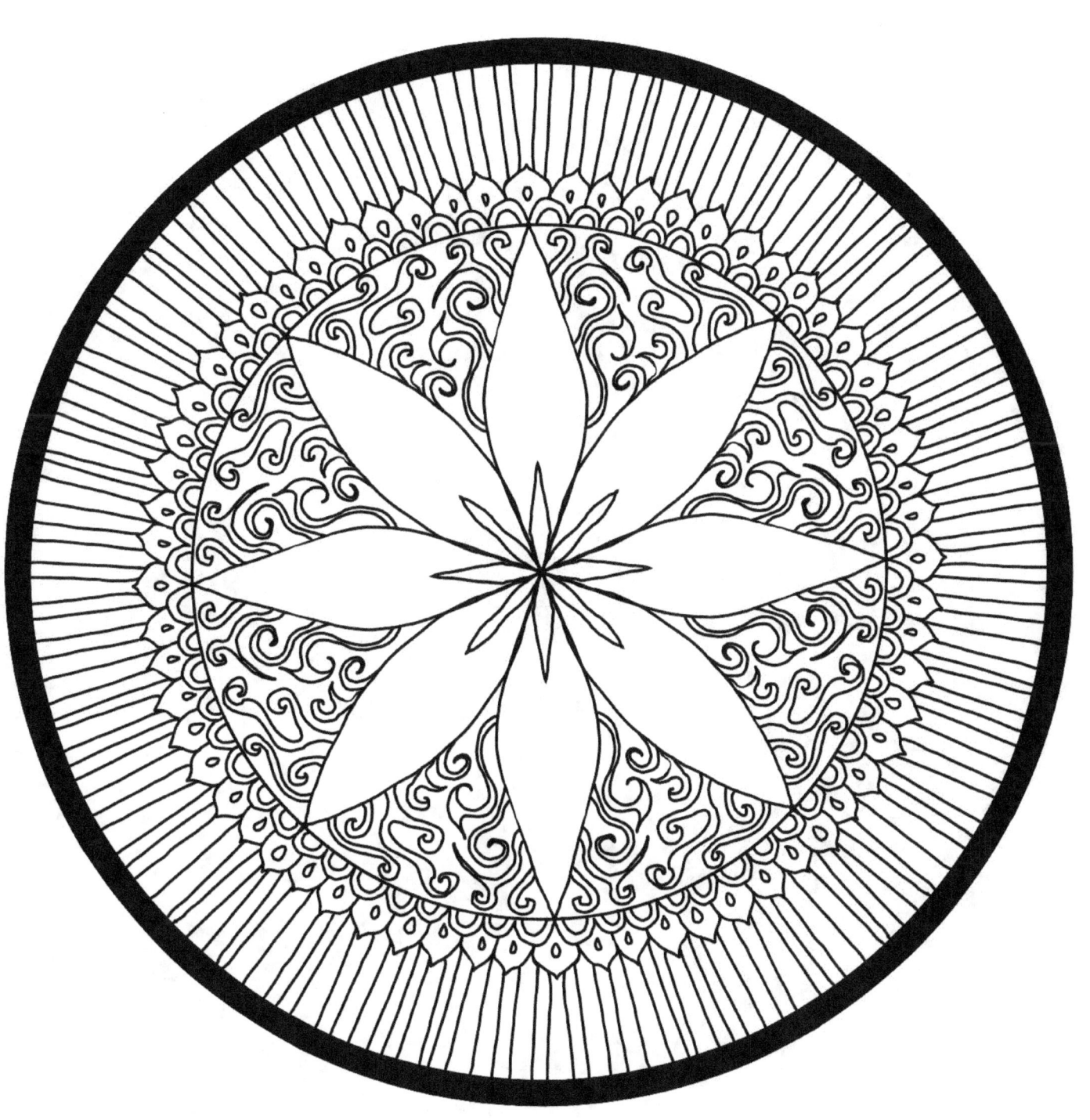

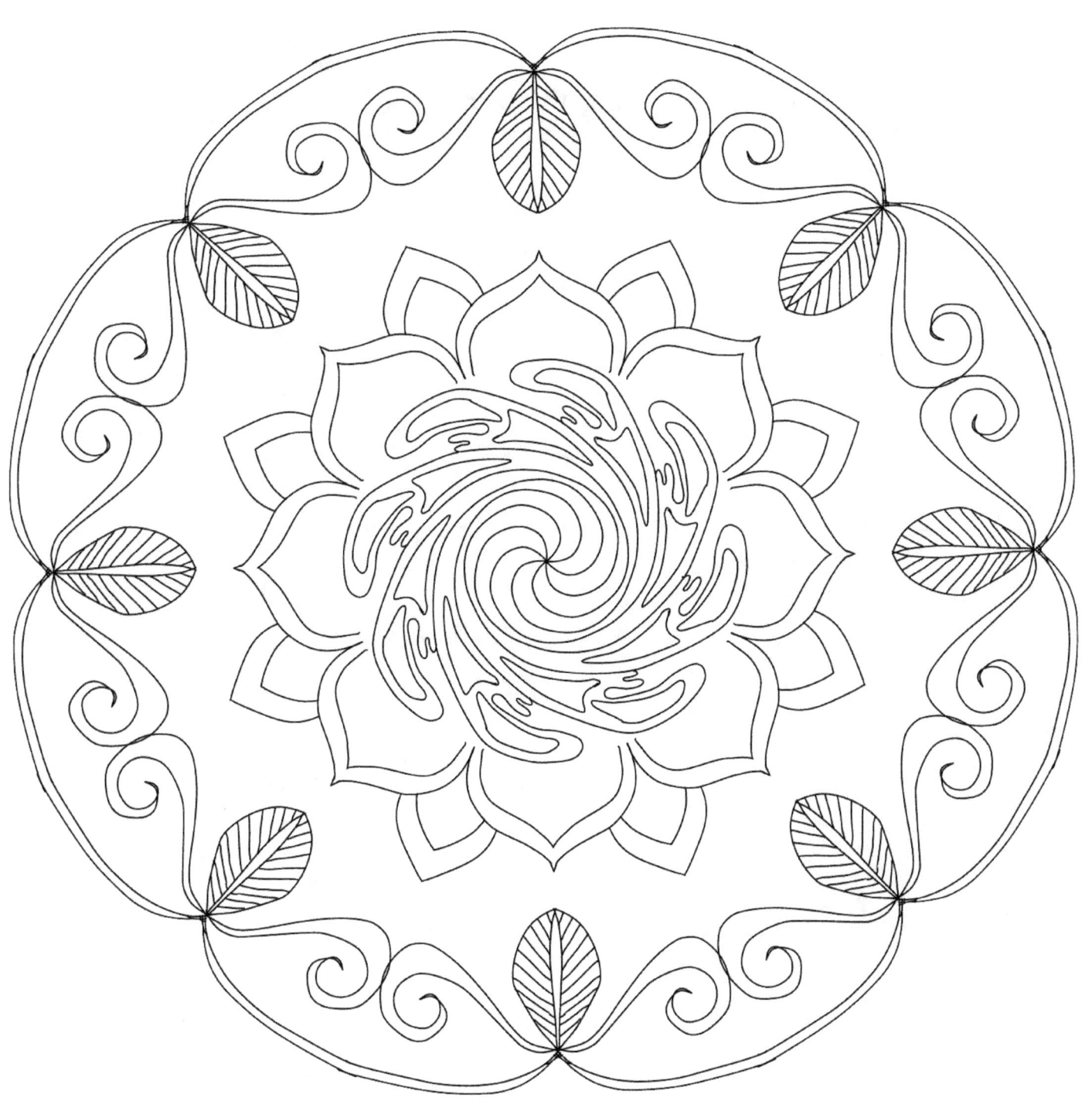

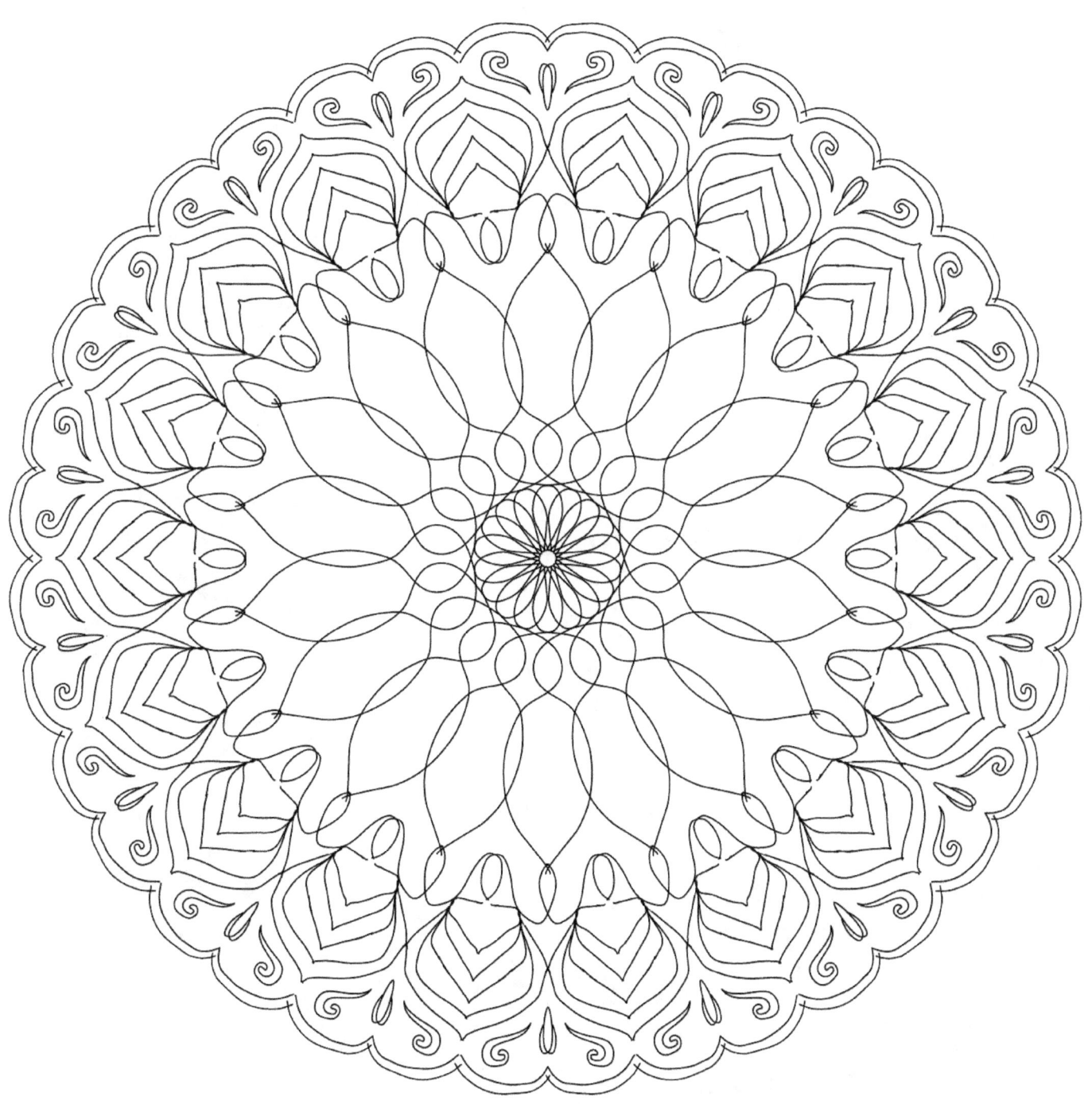

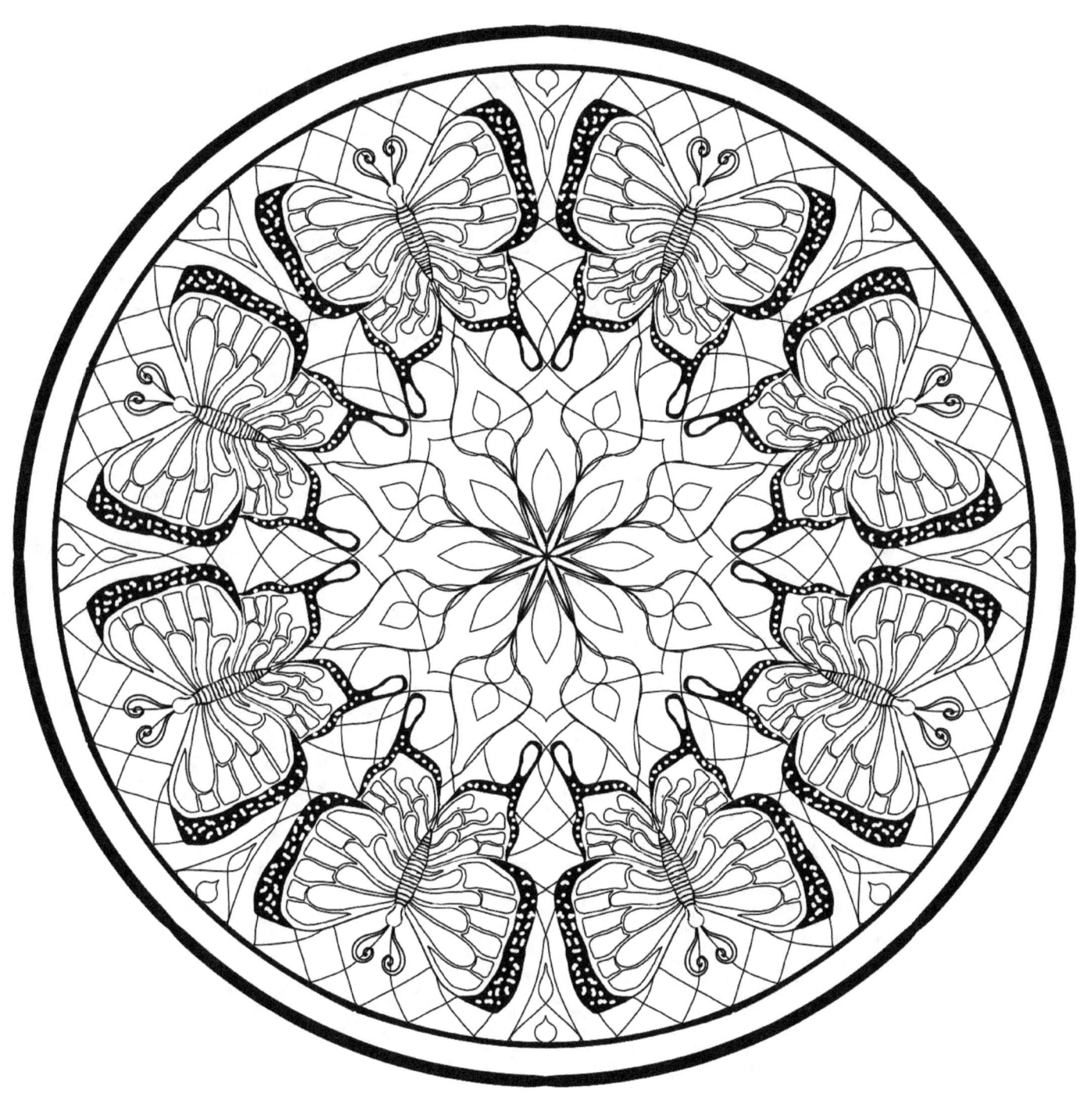

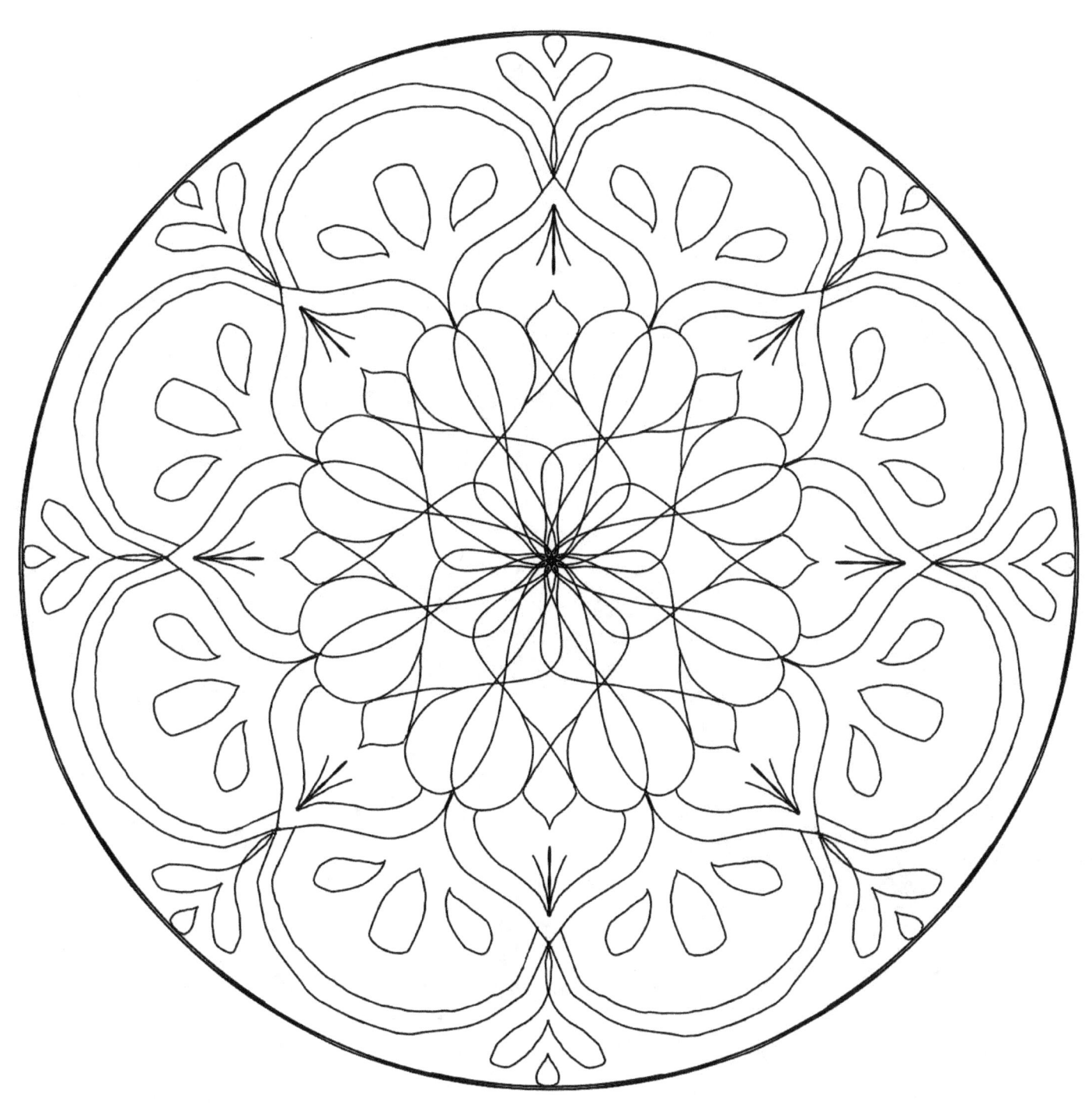

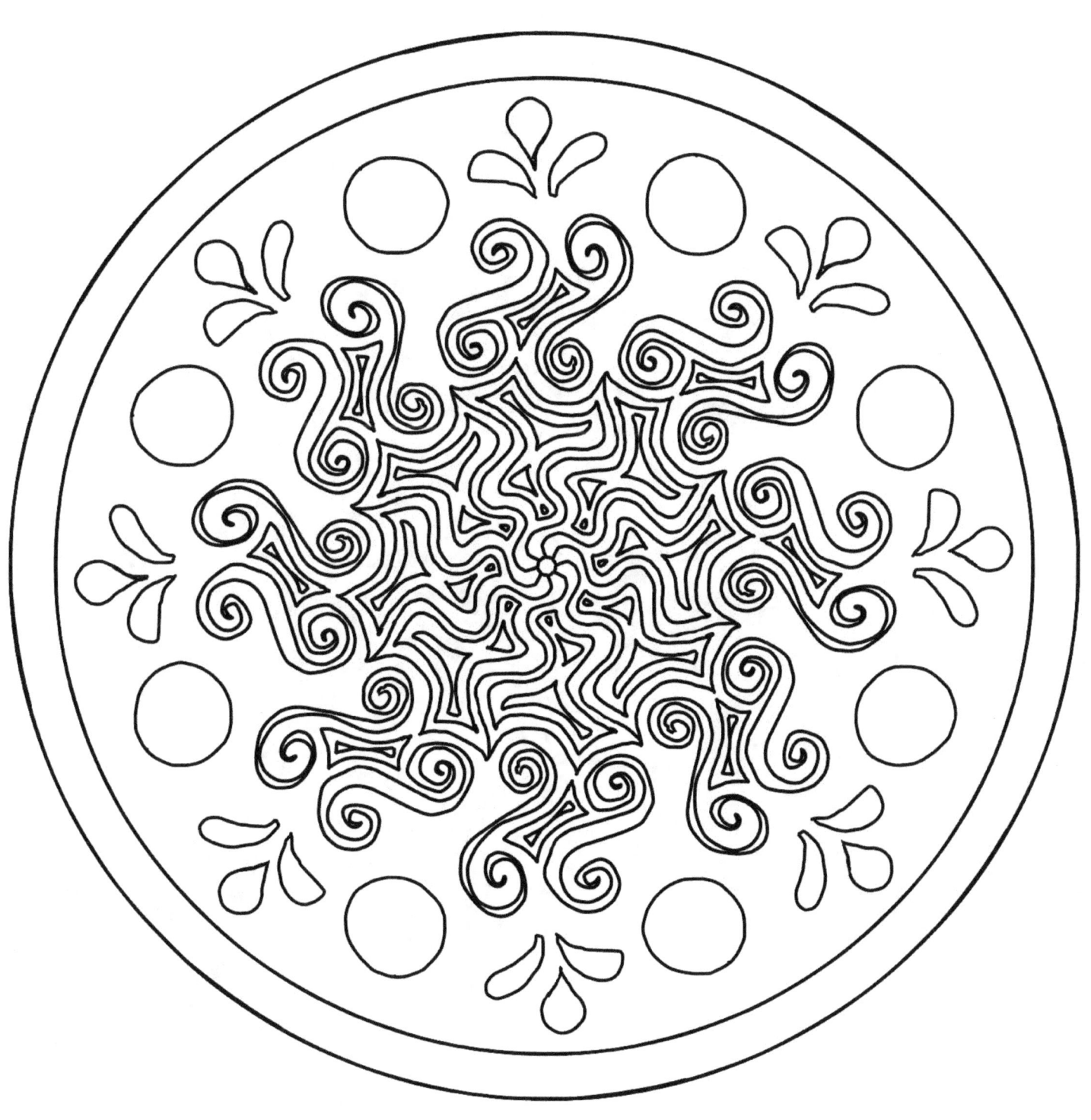

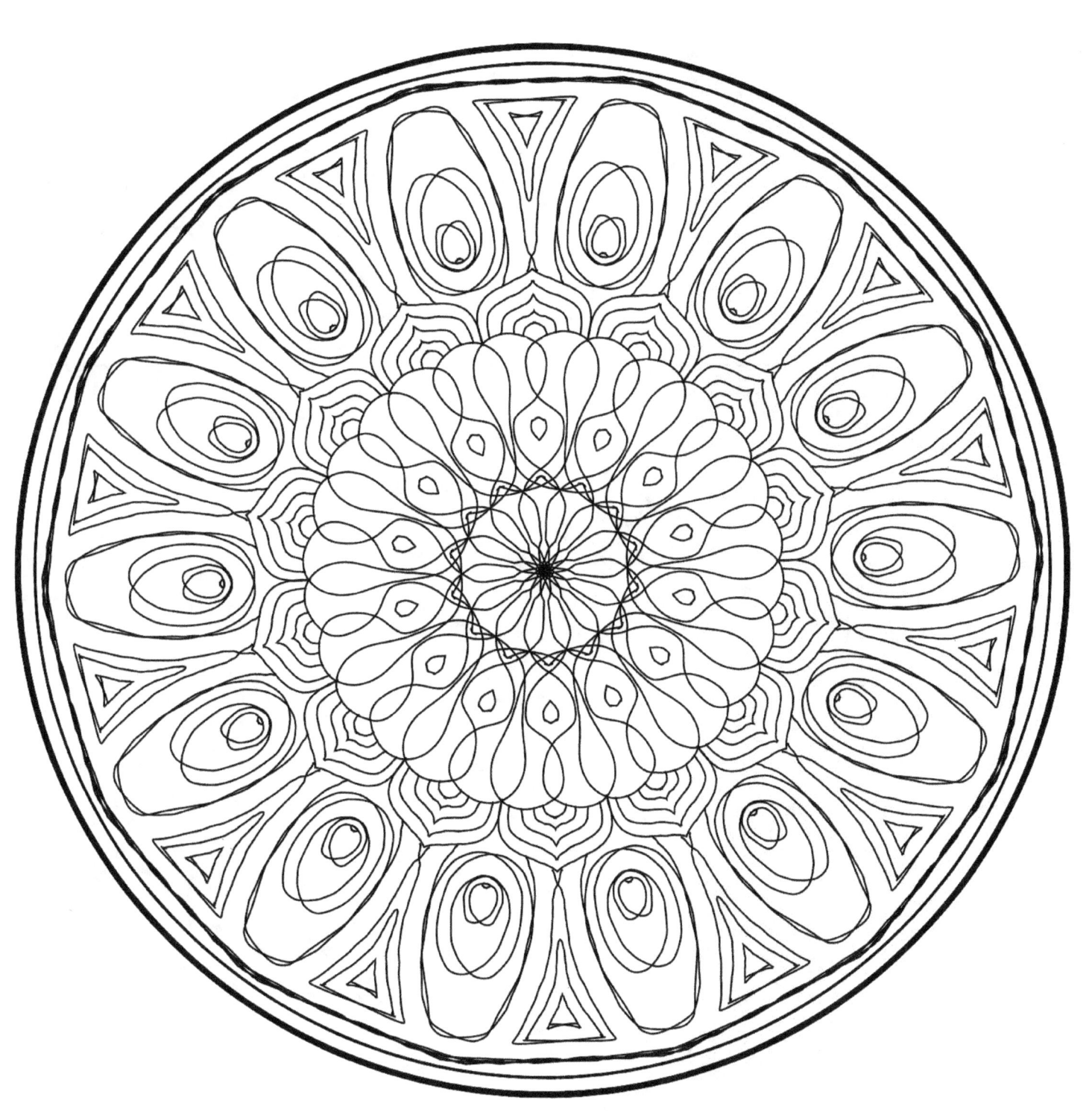

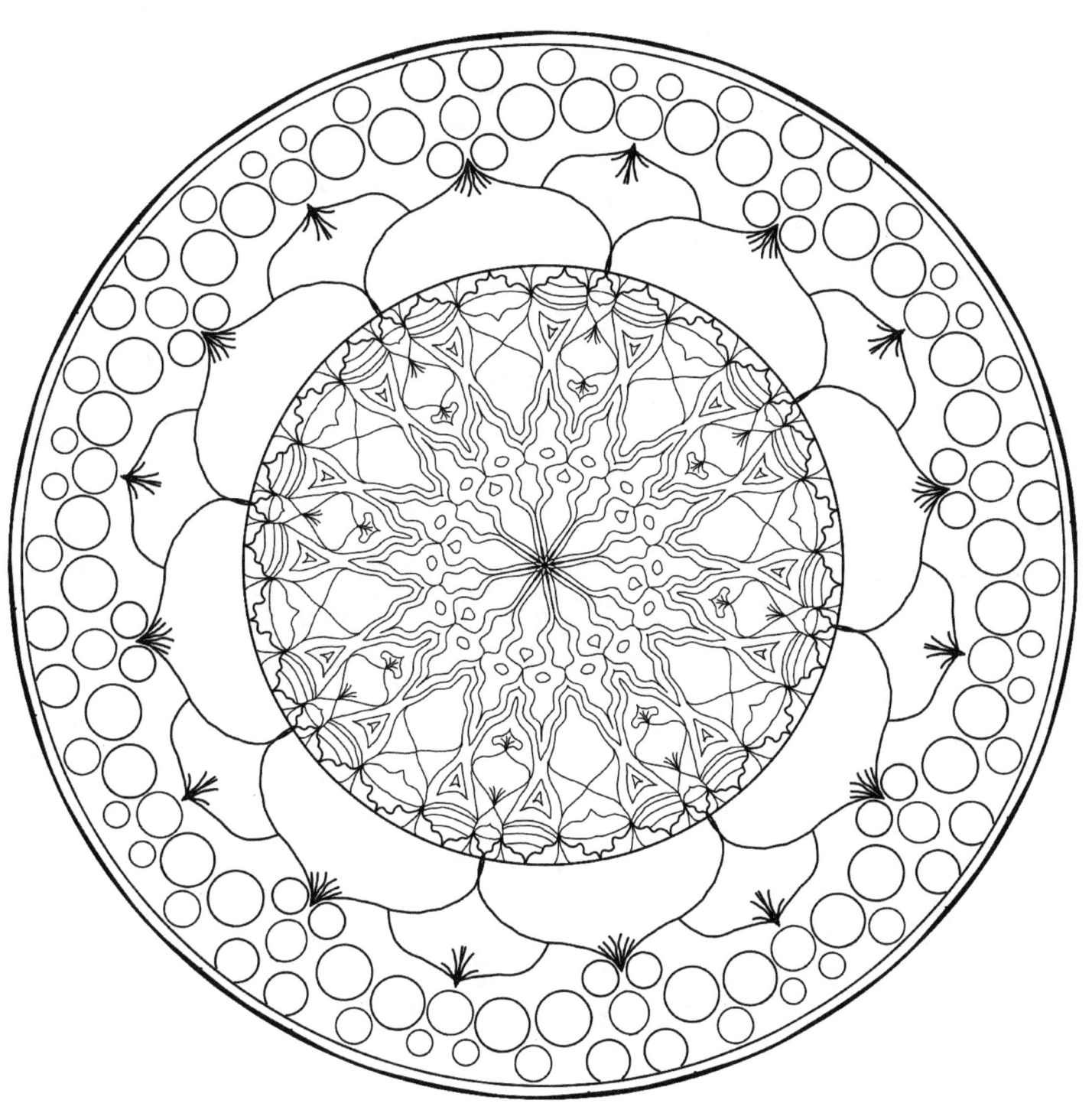

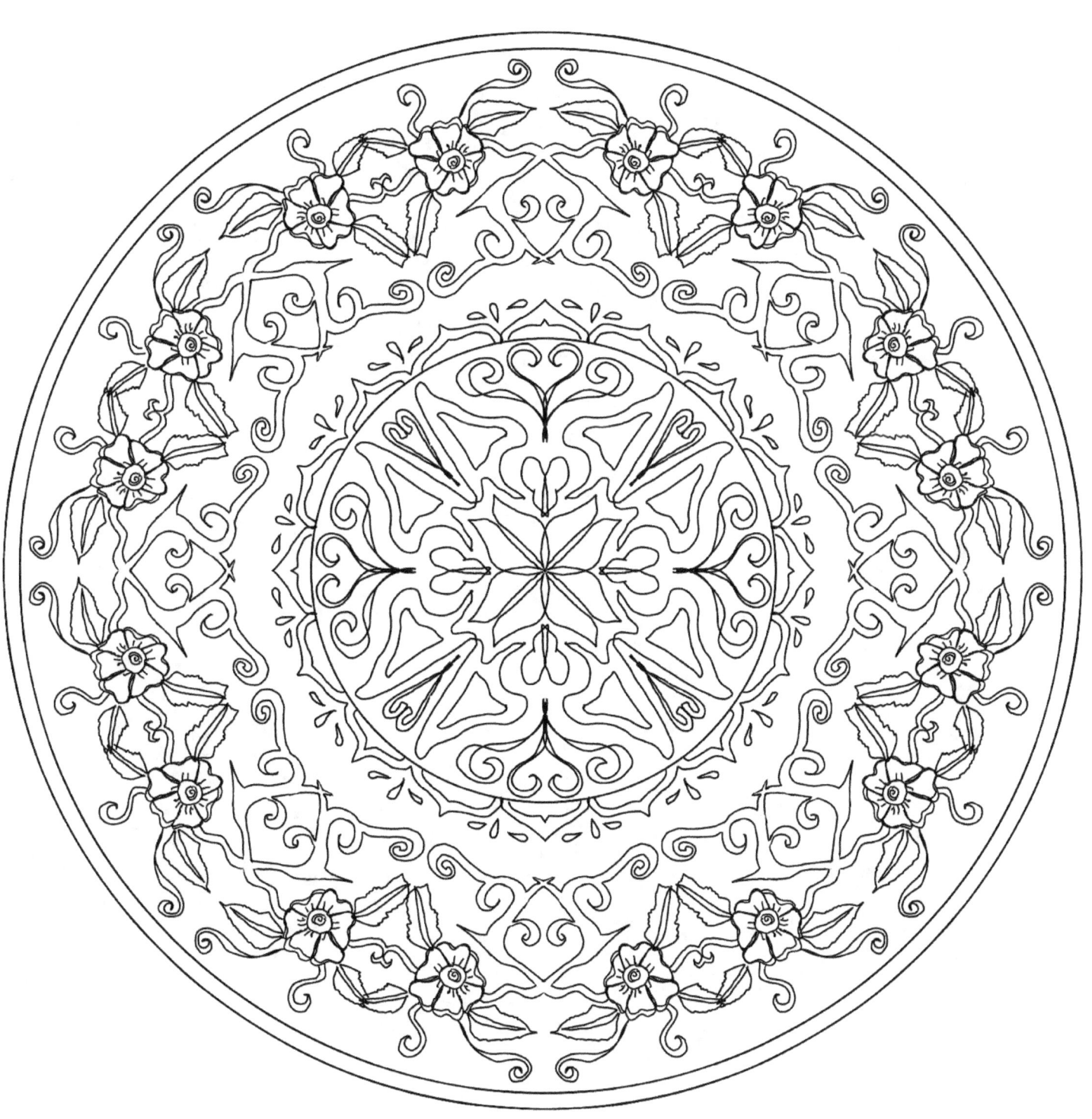

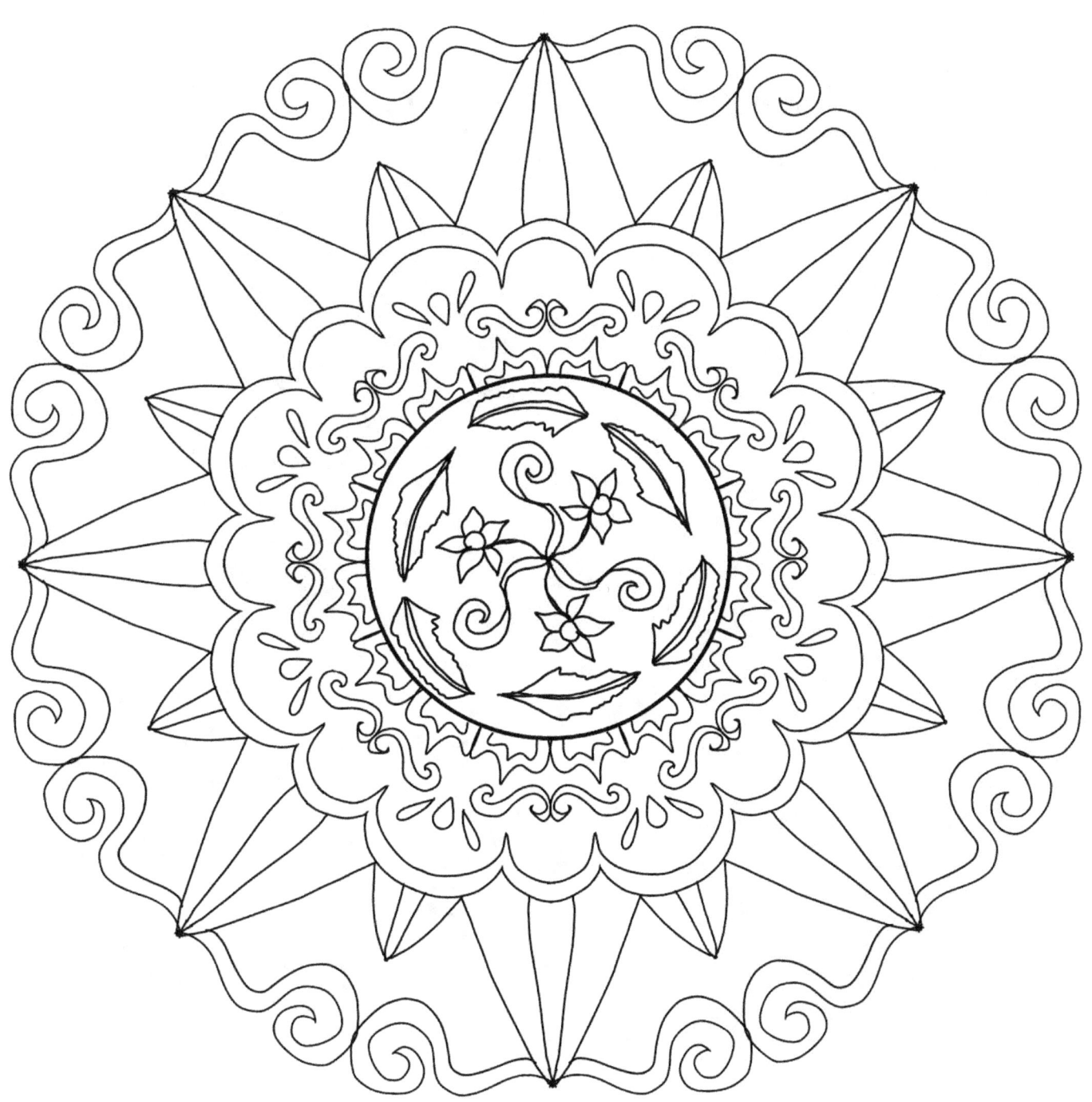

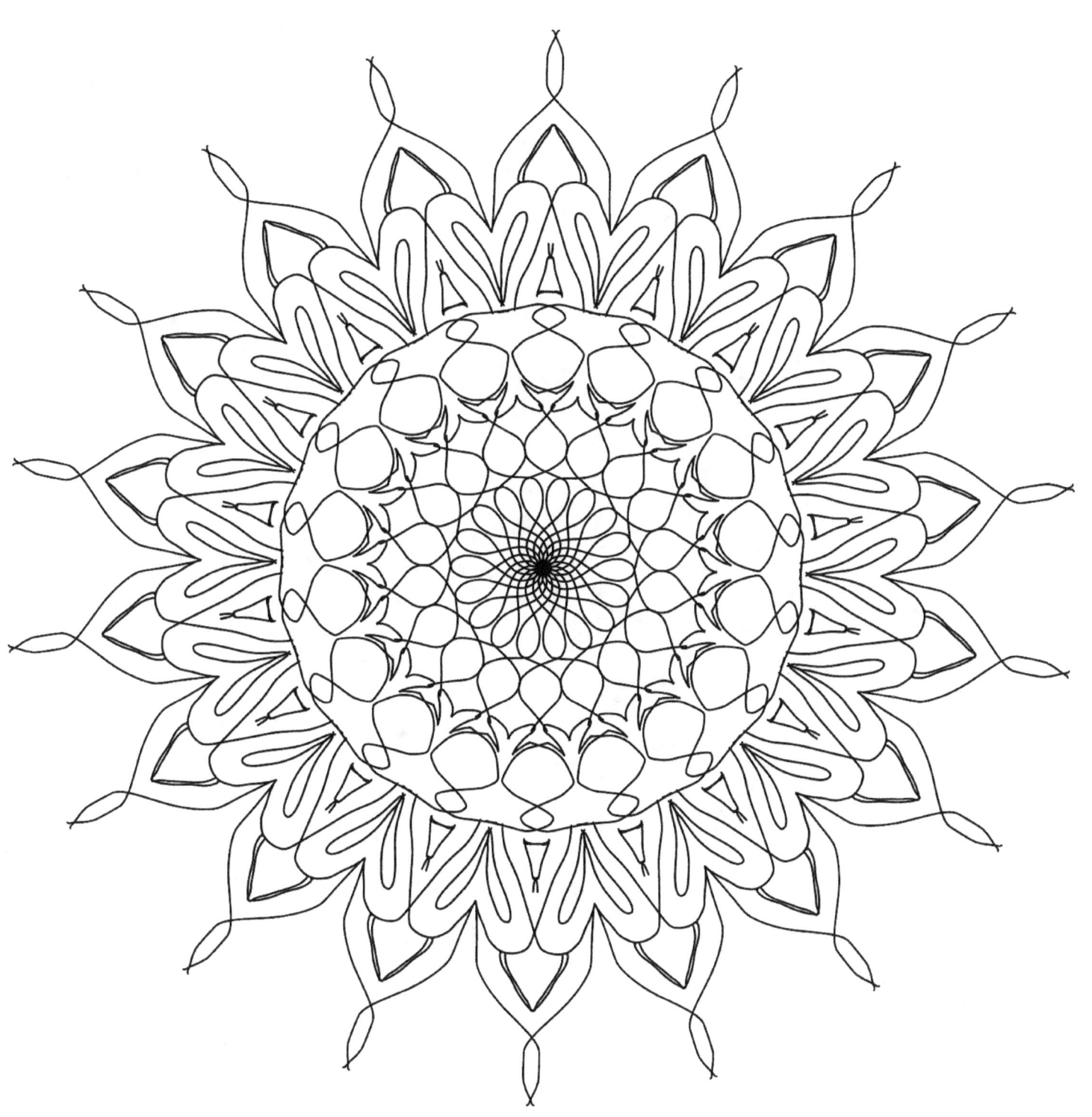

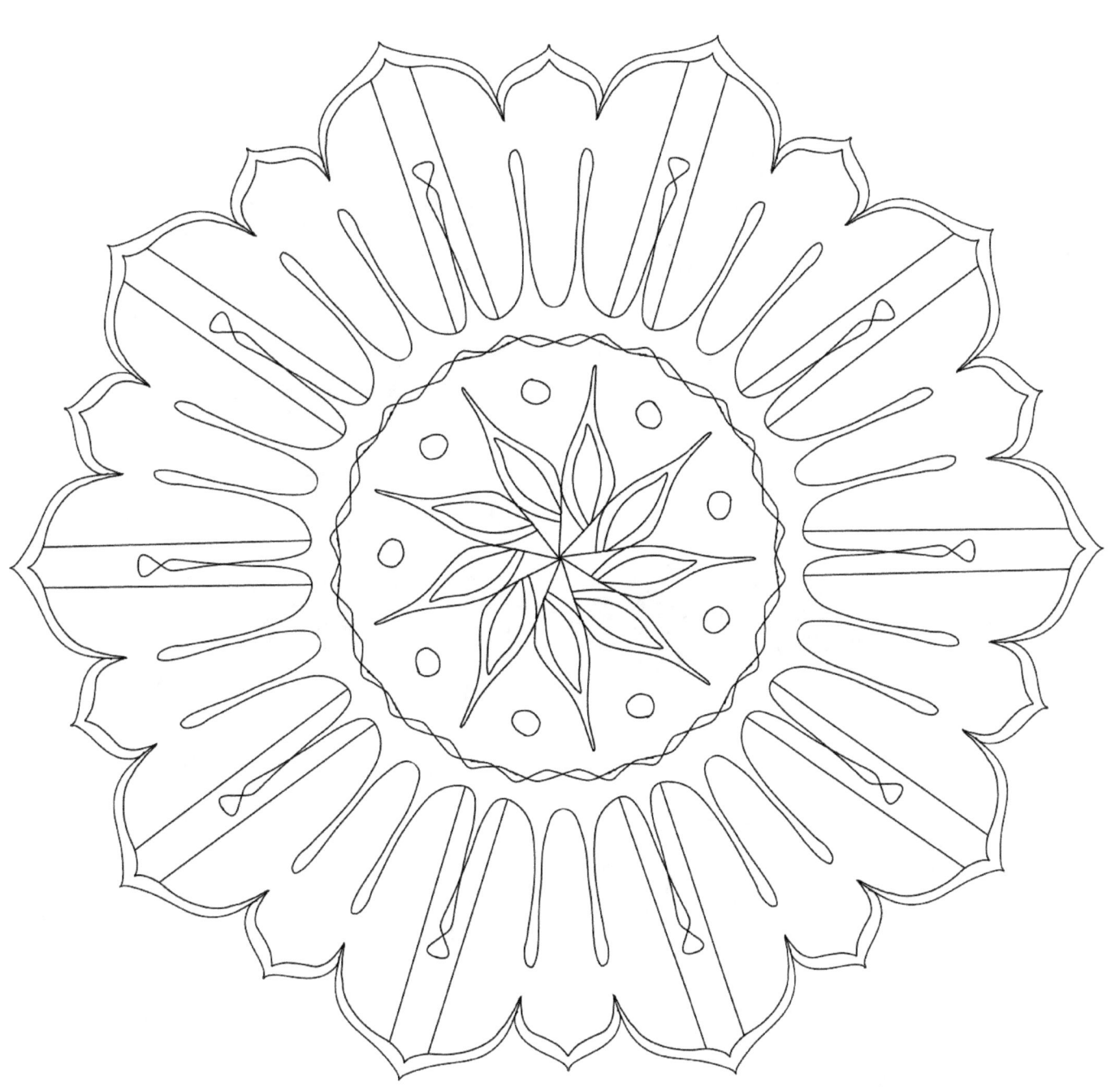

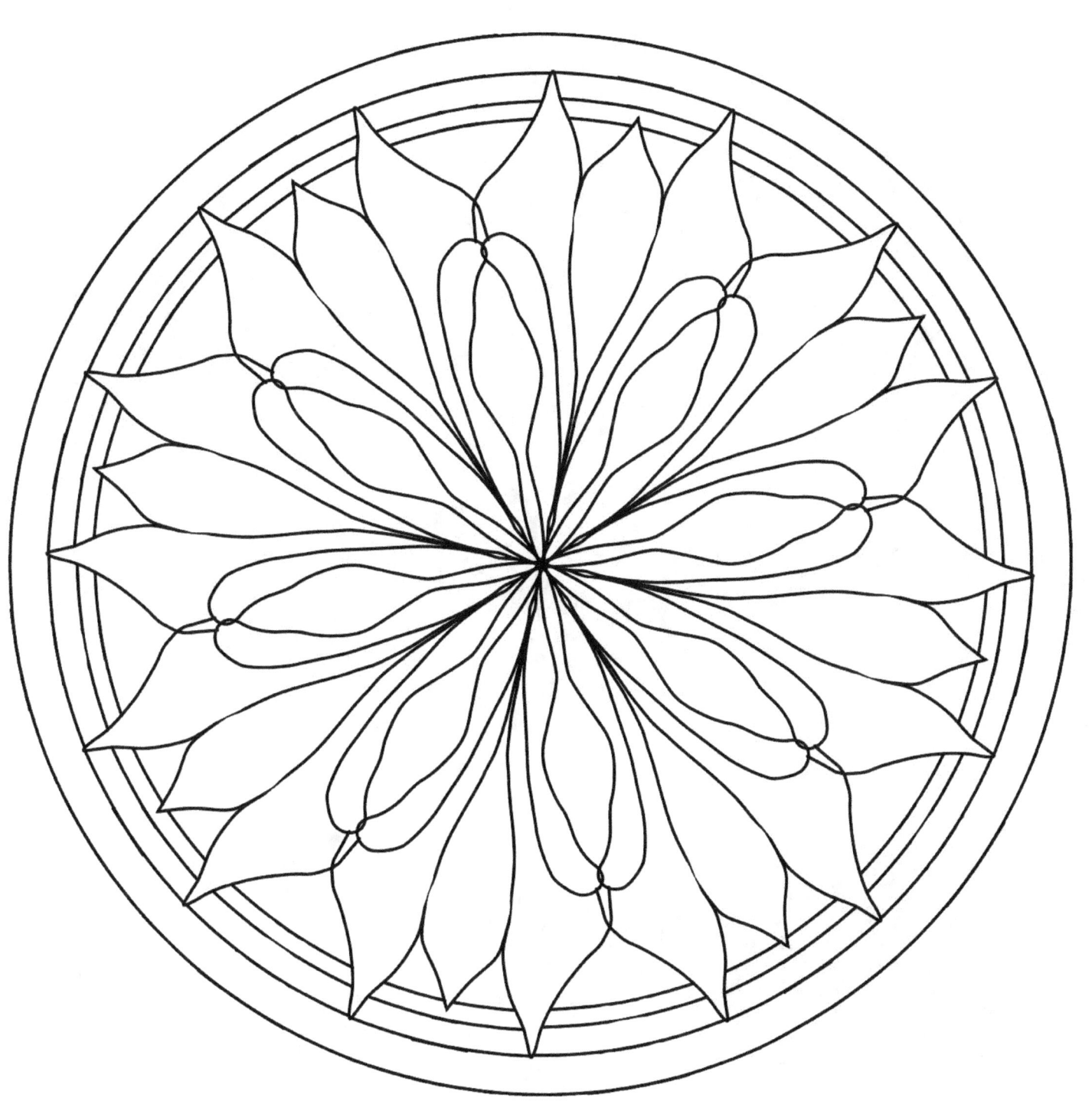

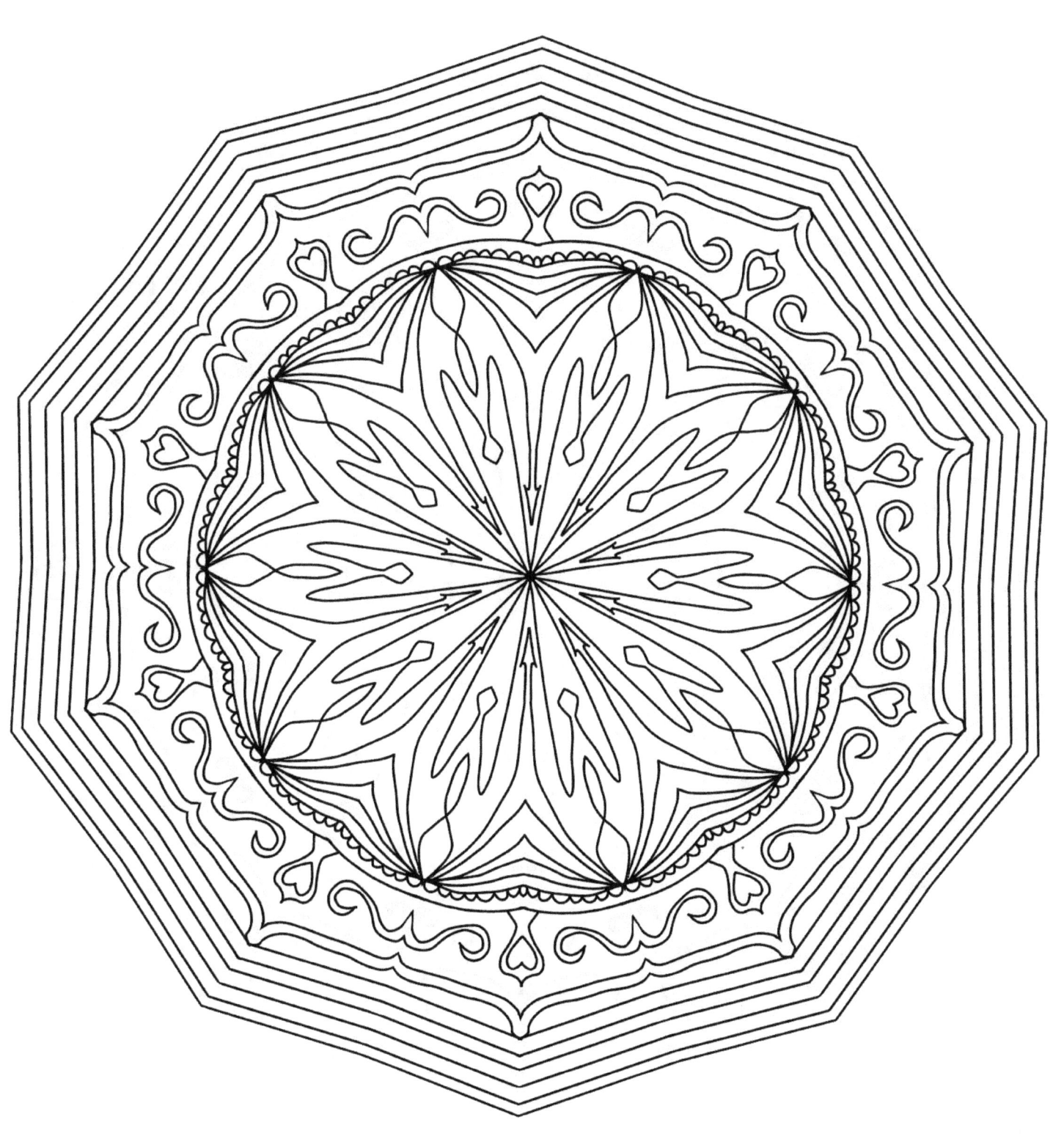

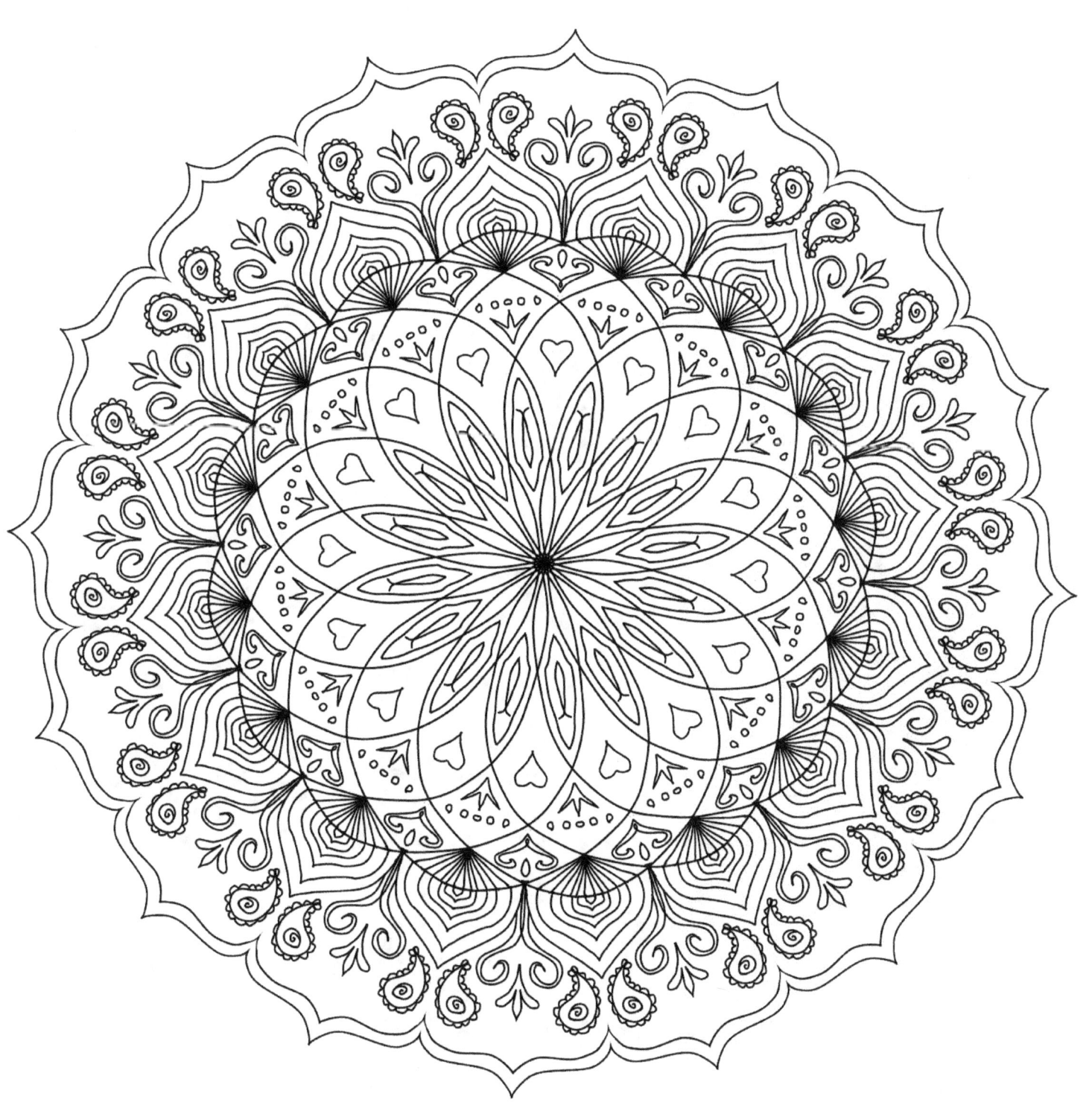

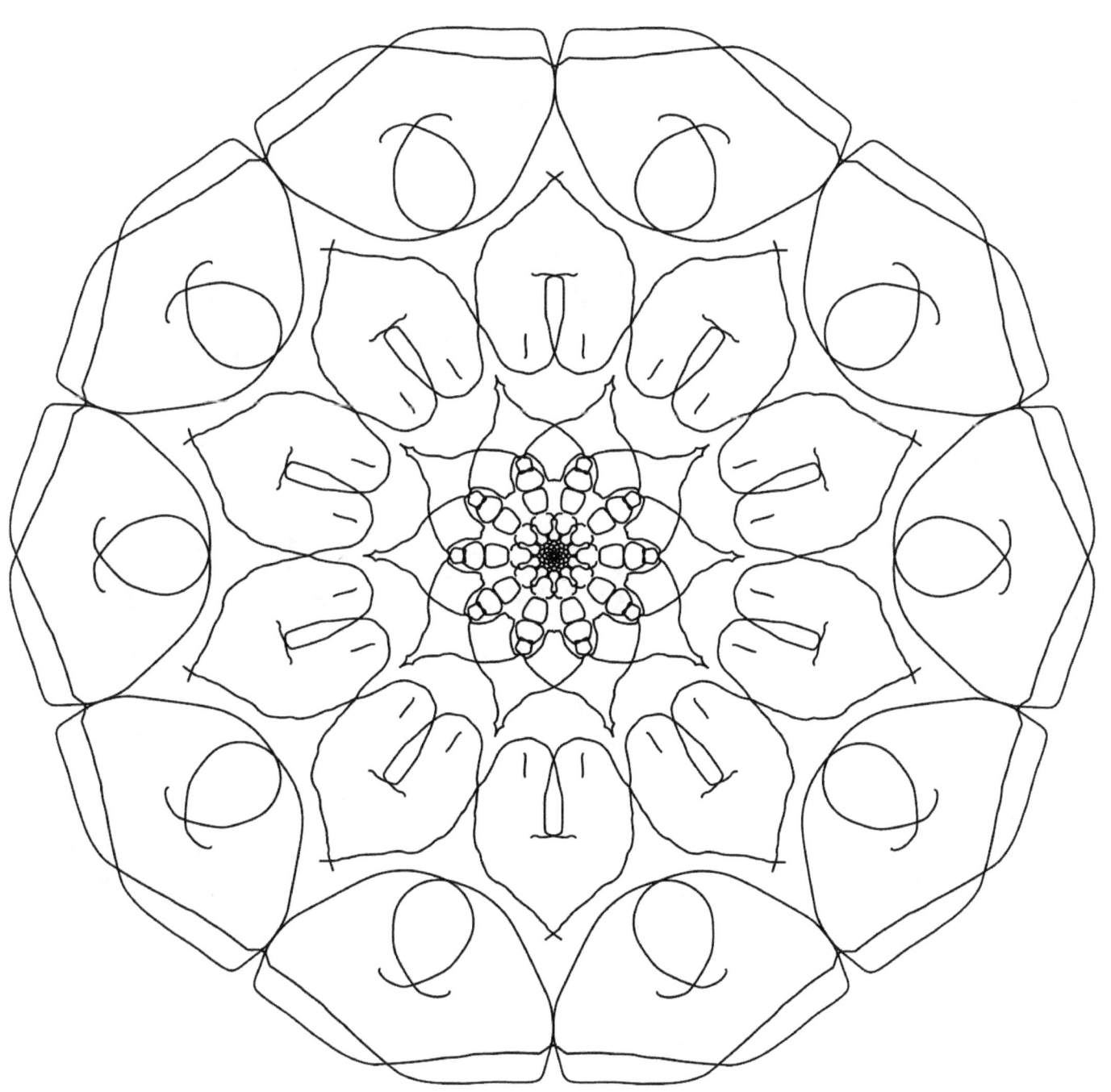

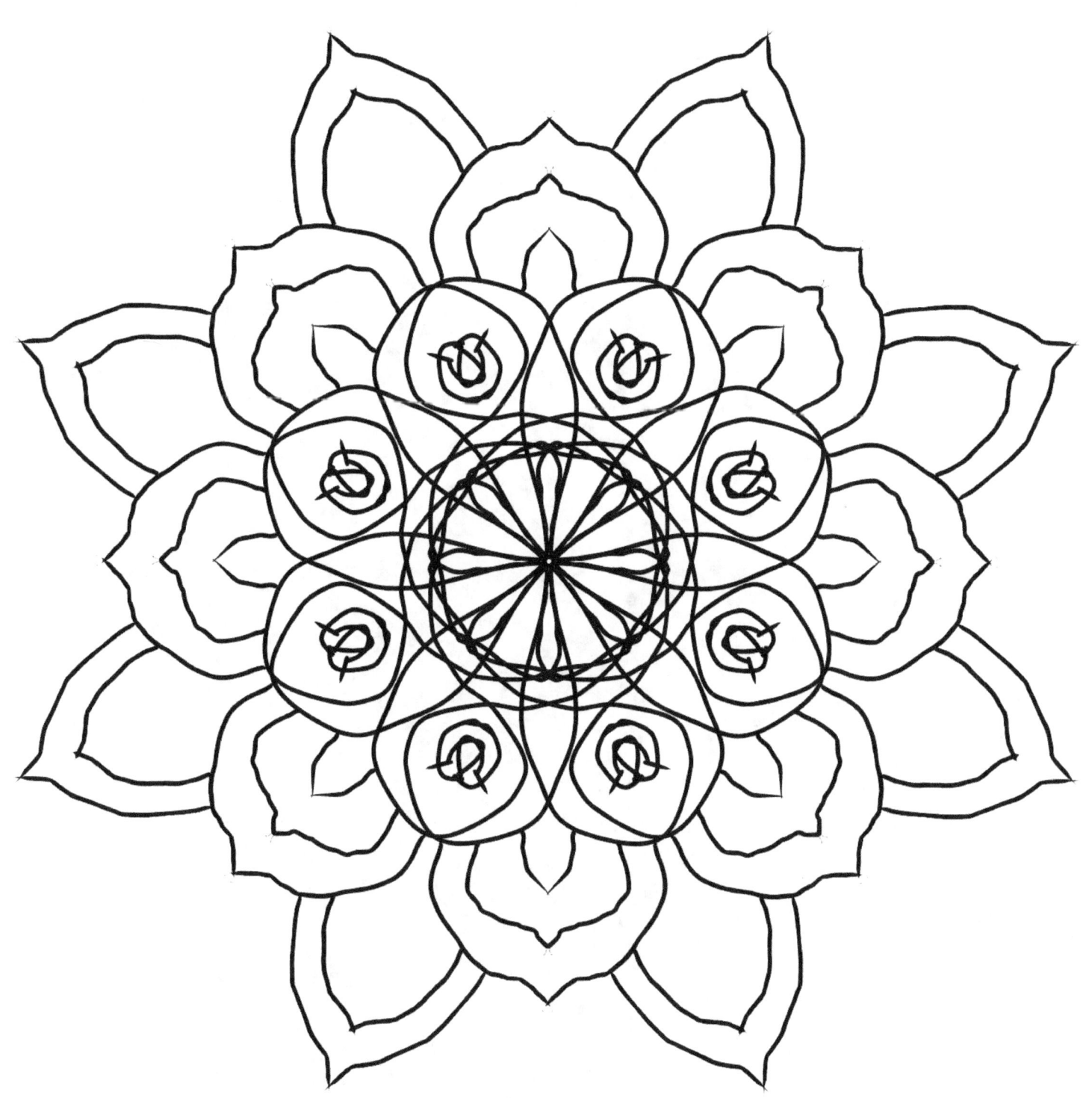

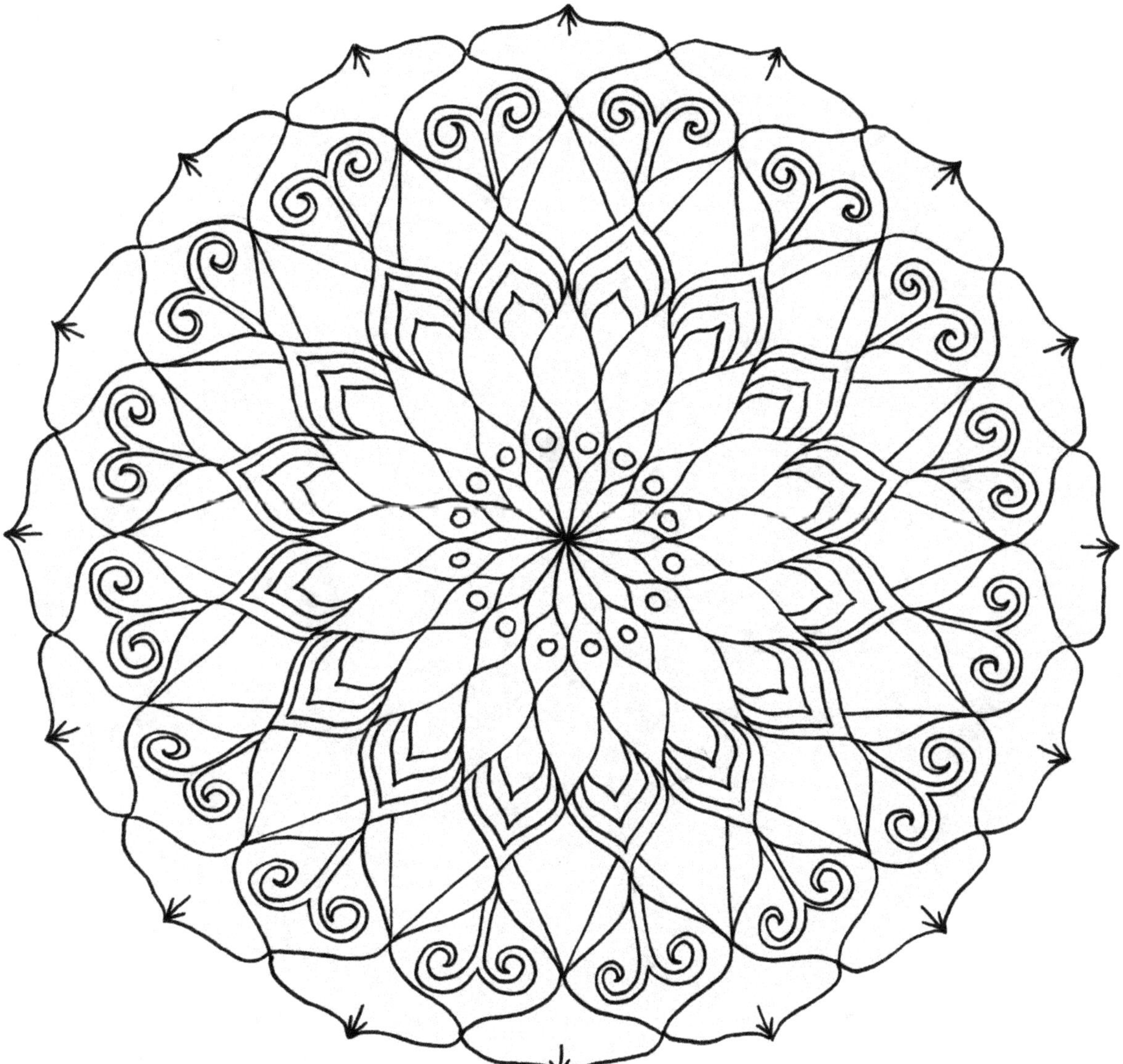

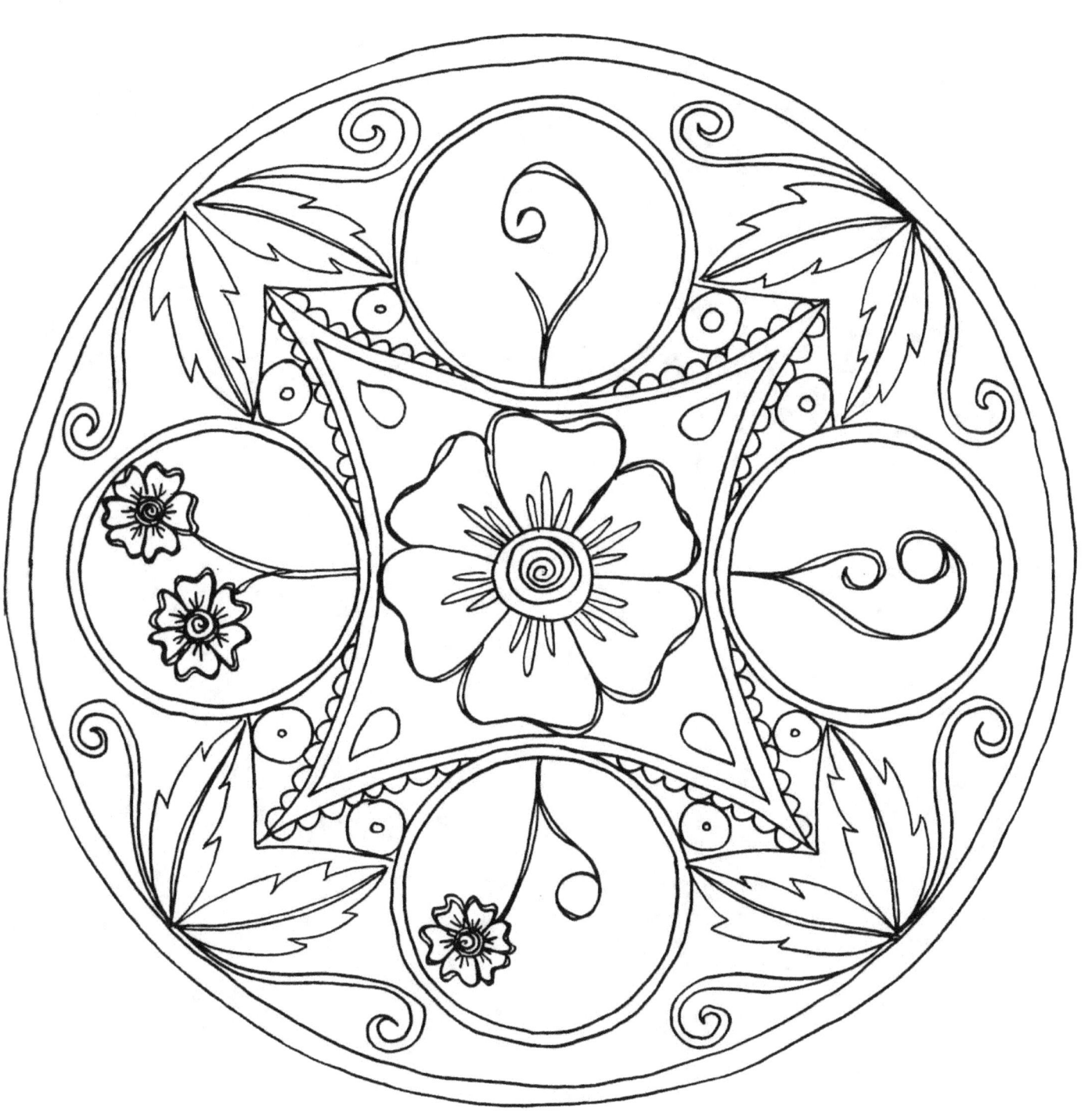

About April

April is a woman of many talents including be-
ing a qualified Acupuncturist, Breastfeeding
Counsellor, Birth Doula, Postnatal Doula,
Childbirth Educator, and trainer for other birth
professionals. She is also a mother of four, an
artist, and musician.

While working with her acupuncture and birth
clients she recognised an increasing need for
patients time out, along with thinking about
where they were going, and what was happen-
ing in their lives.

To fill this need April created a collection of
colouring in books to help people to focus on
the positives in their lives, and to take time out
to rest their minds, while at the same time
create beautiful artwork.

Visit her website www.nurturinglife.com.au to
see what other books are also available.

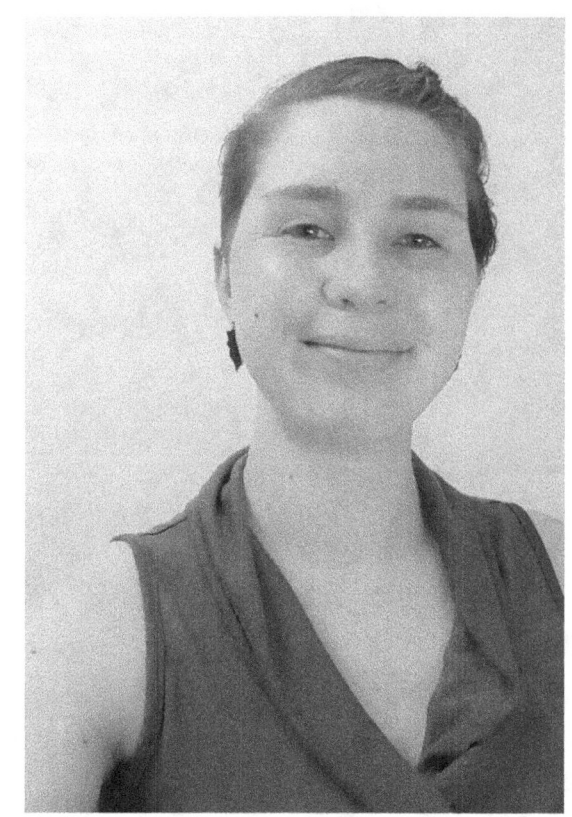

Connect with me

Follow and tag me on Instagram: @birthmandala

Please feel free to tag me or use #birthmandala in
any images you post of finished coloured in pictures
(or Instagram). I love seeing what everyone does with
the pictures!

www.ingramcontent.com/pod-product-compliance
Lightning Source LLC
Chambersburg PA
CBHW081623170526
45166CB00009B/3079